# Summary of

# Dr. Gundry's Diet Evolution

## By Dr. Steven Gundry

## Smart Reads

D1218242

Note to readers:
This is an unofficial summary & analysis of
Dr. Steven Gundry's "Dr. Gundry's Diet
Evolution" designed to enrich your reading
experience. The original book can be
purchased on Amazon.

# Download Your Free Gift

As a way to say "Thank You" for being a fan of our series, I've included a free gift for you:

Brain Health: How to Nurture and Nourish Your Brain For Top Performance

Go to www.smart-reads.com to get your FREE book.

The Smart Reads Team

# Table of Contents

## Overview of *Dr. Gundry's Diet Evolution*

*Dr. Gundry's Diet Evolution: Turn Off the Genes That Are Killing You and Your Waistline* details the exact program that has changed the lives of so many of Dr. Steven Gundry's patients. And in three stages, he explains how you can do the same.

Gundry's background is in heart surgery, and he had become accustomed to "fixing" the body's warning signs in his patients through drug prescriptions and surgeries. In 2001, however, everything changed for him. He met a patient who had reversed severe and inoperable arterial damage simply by changing his diet. Gundry then began studying the effects of diet through a human evolutionary biology lens and started to develop the Diet Evolution. As he worked with patient after patient, guiding them through the program, he consistently saw the same results: completely regained health, along with substantial weight loss. He left his position as a cardiothoracic professor and department chair to build a new career advocating this new-found knowledge.

The premise of the program is simple:

Human genes evolved over time to make certain specific interpretations about you based on the foods that you consume. Your genes' #1 objective is to preserve and propagate the species — and you are either helping that endeavor, or you're hindering it.

The foods you eat, meanwhile, act like keys that unlock certain codes in your genes. Just like the Internet is vast and essentially limitless in what you can do with it — your genes hold nearly infinite possibility. And just like typing an address into a Web browser, which tells your computer where specifically to go, the food you eat tells your genes what specifically to do.

The modern diet sends messages to your genes that indicate that you are interfering with the continuation of the species. Consequently, your genes unleash killer processes that cause you to deteriorate more quickly.

By reversing your diet backward in time — so that it more closely resembles that of our early ancestors — you can send new signals to your genetic autopilot that shuts down those killer processes and turns on life-giving processes.

The Diet Evolution is a three-phase program that gradually transitions you from a modern diet to a largely plant-based, raw diet.

## Chapter 1: Your Genes Are Running the Show

Gundry opens the book by discussing what he sees as the fundamental nature of your genes: that they serve one purpose — the continuation of the species. When it comes to your personal health and lifespan, your genes interpret incoming signals (delivered, in part, by the foods you eat) and judge accordingly whether you're a net positive force or a net negative force for the continuation of the species. When it appears that you're a net positive, then your genes unlock codes that support your health; when it appears that you're a net negative, then your genes unlock codes that harm you — what Gundry refers to as your "killer genes."

In order to accomplish the perpetuation of the species, there are three things our genetic autopilot guides us to do:

- Find and conserve energy (obtain adequate calories with the least expenditure of effort)
- Avoid injury and pain
- Find pleasure

Note that sugar, fat, and salt are three rapid mechanisms by which we achieve all three of these pursuits.

These three personal pursuits are not for our own sake, however. They're meant to serve the continuation of your genetic line. Ultimately, your genes "want" you to achieve three things in your existence:

1. Deliver genes into the future by reproducing.

2. Ensure the survival of your genetic copies or other similar copies.
3. After accomplishing #1 and #2, get out of the way so you don't compete for limited resources with your offspring.

The mechanisms of finding and conserving energy, avoiding injury and pain, and finding pleasure are meant to facilitate our effectiveness in propagating the genetic line. Because they do so with such rapidity, however, they move us into the third step (i.e. get out of the way) more quickly. In other words, they cause us to die faster.

This raises questions about our theories on aging and death. The former "wear and tear" theory, which supposed that the use of the body was what wears it down until it can't handle living anymore, has been debunked by recent research. Instead, it seems that aging and death are "ordered" to take place. This command is given by your "killer genes."

When you defy any of your three key objectives in existence, especially #3, your killer genes are activated. Some specific behaviors that activate these genes include:

- Overeating (because that indicates that you're being selfish, taking too much away from others in your species, violating goal #3)
- Inactivity (because that indicates that you aren't a contributing member of society, violating goal #2)
- Over-exercising (because that indicates that you *have* to work harder to get calories — which indicates that you're an unsuccessful animal, and therefore there's no point in carrying on your genes)

- Smoking (which causes oxidative stress, triggering the same indicators as over-exercising)
- Living on foods full of refined grains, sugar, and trans fats and deficient in micronutrients (because that indicates you're eating more than your fair share, violating goal #3)

When you eat foods containing sugar, fat, and salt, your genes interpret them as the best of the best. Initially, they were good for you because they helped ensure your health and ability to propagate. But after a while, if you're still consuming them, your genes say, "Wait a second. Stop eating all the best stuff. You have offspring who need some of that too, and you're taking too much."

Your body does this by means of a "program" that monitors the number of calories you consume and compares that to a standard that allows each human to grow, reproduce, raise children, and then get out of the way.

This reflects a phenomenon known as Genetic Plietrophy, which states that "genes that activate one sequence of events during part of the life cycle activate the opposite events when called upon to change direction." In other words, our modern foods are so "good" for you that they become bad for you.

The effects of the modern diet are so predictable, in fact, that it's come to be known as the "Rule of Twenty Years." When a primitive culture adopts the Western diet, particularly refined carbohydrates, within only one generation its people begin to experience the typical diseases of the civilized world. Hypertension, diabetes, heart disease, arthritis, cancer, and colitis — diseases currently unknown or rare in such cultures — all become rampant.

The Diet Evolution program was designed to address these genetic messages directly. As you progress through the program, you'll begin to:

1. Fool your genes into thinking that you're not fat enough to kill yet.

2. Convince them you're not working overtime, struggling to survive.
3. Get them to reverse their effect so they undo the damage that they — with your help — have already done to your body.

Feeding your body what is good for *you* and eliminating what is bad for you will get your genes back on your team.

## Chapter 2: We Are What We Eat

This chapter overviews the historical evolution of the human diet (in response to new technologies), discusses outcomes found in modern plant-based and meat-based diets, and looks at some of the basic components of nutrition and health.

First, Gundry looks at four stages in the evolutionary timeline of the human diet:

1. Early humans' diet
2. The hunter-gatherer diet
3. The diet of the Agricultural Revolution
4. The modern diet

For most of human history, we subsisted mostly on plants. There's no evidence that animals were ever the dominant food source until very recent history. Even when humans were getting most of their *calories* from animal products, they relied primarily on plant material to fill their stomachs.

As time progressed, we moved from subsisting on micronutrient-dense and calorie-sparse food to calorie-dense and micronutrient-sparse foods.

As our ancestors began eating a more omnivorous "Hunter-Gatherer" diet (roughly 150,000 years ago), they experienced sturdier bone structure and taller stature (as a result of a more optimal combination of calories and micronutrients). This change also led to more free time than the previous purely herbivorous diet.

The Agricultural Revolution (roughly 10,000 years ago), with its domestication of animals, made access to animals as food much easier. At the same time, grain production dramatically altered the way we ate: grains are easier to store and transport and could be cultivated in most environments, leading to their rapid adoption as a diet staple. What's more, they're both micronutrient-dense and calorie-dense, delivering more nutrition and energy in fewer bites (a big win for Rule #1 of genetic survival, i.e. to maximize energy intake).

The diet following the Agricultural Revolution was overall very similar to our modern diet, with one notable exception: the animals consumed then were raised grazing on grasslands and prairie, and therefore were rich in micronutrients, which were passed onto the humans who ate the animals. Contrast this with today's animals, which are fattened up on grain and corn and pass on far fewer micronutrients.

In the modern diet (from roughly 1900 to the present), we've dramatically changed our diets to include lots of grain (most of it refined), an increase in animal meat (which were raised on even more grain), tons of sugar — and at the same time, we've steadily reduced our consumption of micronutrient-rich plants.

Meanwhile, Western societies have completely transitioned (within only the last 2-3 generations) from death by starvation to death by obesity.

The Diet Evolution program guides you through a reversal of the transformation described above, rejecting grains and processed foods, and moving you gradually through an animal-based (or vegetarian protein alternative) diet into a more plant-based and raw diet.

He explains that both a meat-heavy diet and a plant-based diet can be the right best option... although not in the same phases of health restoration (more on this later).

As you move to a more plant-based diet, you'll do so slowly. One reason for this is that raw plants contain toxins. These toxins actually benefit us, but if you try to do too much too fast, your liver won't be able to adapt quickly enough.

He shares some other good-to-know characteristics of each type of diet...

With regard to meat-heavy diets:

- Animal protein and grains lead to **more and faster physical growth**. In societies where the population consumes more of these foods, people tend to be taller, and women reach puberty earlier. These societies also tend to have **shorter lifespans**.
- Even herbivores inadvertently consume animals or animal products in the form of grubs, worms, and insects found on the leaves they eat. In zoos, where the leaves fed to animals are washed clean, herbivores' diets need to be fortified with **6% animal protein** in order for them to remain healthy.
- Breaking down animal protein generates a lot of heat in the digestive tract. **In the short-term, this supports weight loss efforts for most people.**

And with regard to plant-based diets:

- The toxins in plants actually promote health through a process called **hormesis** (more on this later in the book).
- Breaking down animal protein, especially muscle, generates a lot of heat in the digestive tract and induces oxidative damage, which induces rapid aging. **This does not occur when digesting plants.**
- Animal products often come with a high **caloric load.**
- Plants are substantially more dense in **micronutrients** than animal protein.

Before moving on, he points out that obesity is not a genetically predisposed outcome of a healthy diet and lifestyle. With the exception of animals that hibernate or anticipate periods of seasonal starvation, there are no overweight animals. Their genetic code won't allow obesity to occur, because — when the animal has adequate stores of fat — the animal's internal monitoring system shuts off hunger signals.

The remainder of the chapter is devoted to some lite education on the primary nutritional components of foods.

First, calories and micronutrients:

**Calories** are not all the same. Calorie counts tell us only how much energy is contained in a food, *not* how much energy your body can derive from it. Calorie counts also don't tell you anything about the micronutrients contained in a food item.

**Micronutrients** are vitamins, minerals, trace elements, phytochemicals (phyto = "plant"), and thousands of other compounds found in some foods. Micronutrients tell your genes to turn on/off or to perform other functions like making proteins, fats, and hormones.

Next, he discusses **Omega-3s** and **Omega-6s**:

- These are the main building blocks of our hormone systems.
- Omega-3s help constructs anti-inflammatory hormones (like prostacyclins and prostaglandins).
- Omega-6s help constructs inflammatory hormones (like arachidonic acid and thromboxanes).
- The ideal ratio between the two appears to be 1:1 or 1:2 (Omega-3:Omega-6).
- On the modern diet, most people have a ratio between 1:20 and 1:40.
- Reflective of this imbalance, some common modern diseases associated with inflammation include arthritis, asthma, skin lesions (psoriasis, eczema), and autoimmune (lupus, multiple sclerosis, Chron's).

And then there's **salt**. If the concentration of salt in your system becomes too low, your cellular machinery stops functioning. And you're constantly losing salt via sweat. Therefore, you're programmed to always be on the lookout for salt to consume. Too much, however, and your body begins to self-destruct.

Up next, **sugar**. Here are three things to know:

- When you eat enough sugar, it causes your pancreas to secrete **insulin** (a growth hormone that tells your body to store sugar as fat) into your bloodstream. As insulin levels rise, a feedback system in the satiety center of your brain is activated.
- Consuming sugar also causes the release of **leptin** (a fat-regulating hormone), which tells your brain you've had enough to eat.
- **Fructose** (fruit sugar) bypasses both of these processes. Rather than entering the bloodstream (which would trigger the release of both hormones), it goes straight to the liver, where it stimulates the production of **triglycerides**, a precursor to **cholesterol**. (Though note that it will still cause insulin to rise, albeit much more slowly.)

This brings us to **insulin**. Insulin has three jobs:

- It delivers sugar and calories to cells for immediate energy production.
- It tells the liver to convert excess sugar into fat for long-term energy storage.
- It stimulates cell growth.

In early human history, the only situation that could lead to a high enough level of insulin for #2 to take place would have been consuming a large amount of fruit. Their genetic autopilots would then correctly assume that it was late summer or early fall and that winter was coming — and insulin would be released to signal the liver to turn sugar into fat so that they could make it through the winter. This is what Gundry refers to as your genetic **"store fat for winter" program**.

Why does our genetic autopilot point us so strongly toward sweet things? Lots of calories, minimal effort. (Remember those three mechanisms at the beginning of the chapter?)

This becomes dangerous with our modern foods, however. Even the *taste* of sweetness raises insulin levels. Some common modern diseases associated with insulin resistance: being overweight, rosacea, and skin tags.

Before closing, Gundry takes a look at grains and legumes.

**Legumes** (which include most beans and lentils) are calorie-dense (many of those from sugars, and they often contain phytates, which slow or prevent the absorption of micronutrients in the intestinal tract. As you move through the program, Gundry typically treats these as part of the same category as grains.

In order to understand **grains**, we first look at a brief history of grain production:

- Grains were introduced approx. 10,000 years ago and brought with them nutrients with which we had probably never before interacted.
- In 1890, the steel roller mill was invented to produce white flour. Unfortunately, this process essentially eradicated all nutritional value (by eliminating oil-rich germs and fiber-rich bran),

contributing to millions of deaths in the early 1900s due to vitamin deficiency.

- In response, a 1920s U.S. federal regulation mandated that white flour be fortified with a minimum of eight essential vitamins and minerals (the same ones the steel-roller mill removed). The resulting product became known as "enriched white flour."

After they've been finely ground and processed, grains are rapidly digested and enter directly into the bloodstream as sugar. This activates the same "store fat for winter" program discussed above.

Gundry ends the chapter with a cautionary story: Baboons, which subsist in the wild on leaves, nuts, fruit, insects, and small animals, normally have low cholesterol and no coronary artery disease. But when they take up residence on hotel grounds and feed off foods discarded by tourists, they grow larger and faster, females hit puberty earlier, they develop high cholesterol, and they die younger of coronary artery disease and other human diseases such as tuberculosis.

## Chapter 3: Changing the Message

Chapter 3's focus is on how you can reverse the damage already done to your system and begin sending new messages to your genetic machine.

Your genes "act" based on the instructions they're handed — and you can start to give them a new set of instructions.

As Gundry writes, "I tell my patients [that] I am the same obese person with the same genetic program who now occupies a thin, fit body — and by the way, I eat more food than I've ever eaten before. But really, I'm not the same person because almost every cell in my body has been replaced with revised, reinvigorated cells... Even though my cells have changed, my genes have not."

The characteristics of the Gundry Diet Evolution program:

First, it's not about controlled perfection. There's no calorie counting, and you can eat as much as you want of certain foods. And, with the exception of the first two weeks (which are fairly strict), you're allowed a lot of flexibility to find what works for you.

Second, the program moves by means of gradual change, in three stages, in order to meet your body's changing needs as you progress.

Finally, rather than make superficial changes, this diet addresses the thing that's really in control: your unseen autopilot. Each stage is tailored to send messages to your genetic autopilot that specifically switch off and on the programs that are relevant for that stage's objectives.

Most diets are simply different variations on modern food. The Gundry Diet is a return to old feeding habits that work and that are sustainable.

Before closing, Gundry shares a foundational concept that he'll return to throughout the book, based in part on the following observations:

1. Plants produce toxins and anti-nutrient phytochemicals... But those phytochemicals are actually good for humans, thanks to the process of hormesis.
2. Animal products and modern processed food are optimized to appeal to your genes — but they also will trigger your genetic "store fat for winter" program.

Thus, Gundry's counterintuitive and oft-repeated phrase that "the things that are 'good' for you are actually bad for you, and the things that are 'bad' for you are actually good for you."

# Chapter 4: The Diet at a Glance

This chapter overviews the entire Diet Evolution program and provides lists of specific foods to eat and to avoid.

**Before getting started**, check in with your physician. Ideally, they'll run some baseline tests, which you can use to monitor your progress over time. Gundry recommends the following tests:

- blood pressure
- heart rate
- fasting glucose level
- hemoglobin A1C
- fasting insulin level
- fasting lipid panel (preferably with fractions of LDL, HDL, Lp(a), Apo B, and Lipo-PLA2)
- homocysteine
- fibrinogen
- C-reactive protein (CRP)

If you're taking blood pressure or blood sugar meds, you may need to be monitored closely by your physician as you go forward.

- By following the Diet Evolution program properly, your blood pressure will normalize — which means you may experience dizziness because your meds are now dropping your blood pressure too low.
- Similarly, your blood sugar levels will experience a natural drop — which also may cause dizziness if you take diabetes pills or give yourself insulin shots.

When you're ready to move on, the three phases of the program are Teardown, Restoration, and Longevity:

**Phase 1: The Teardown**

Purpose: weight loss

Duration: minimum 6 weeks, or continue this phase until you're satisfied with the amount of weight you've lost

Why does it work? During this phase, you're sending to your genes the new signal that "I don't have to store fat for winter."

**Phase 2: Restoration**

Purpose: continuing weight loss and setting your body up for longevity

Duration: minimum 6 weeks, or until your weight normalizes

Why does it work? Here, you're sending the signal that "I'm not a threat to future generations."

**Phase 3: Longevity**

Purpose: lasting health

Duration: this is a lifestyle

Why does it work? You're now sending the signal that "My staying alive ensures my genes' future."

The exciting news is that, because 90% of your existing cells are replaced every three months, you can rapidly build an entirely "new you" by following the program.

## The Case For Supplements

Gundry considers supplementing your diet a form of health insurance.

He writes: "Foraging humans and our ape ancestors usually ate up to 200 different plants on a rotating basis. Today, the rare individual may actually consume 25 plants on a regular basis, but the average American eats about five, and that's including french fries. Moreover, the vast majority of plants are grown with petrochemical fertilizers."

He acknowledges that there's an ongoing debate about the long-term effects of supplements, but writes, "In any debate on supplementation, always remember that most plant compounds are still unnamed, and we don't fully understand how they interact with our genes."

Note that there's an important difference between vitamin **deficiency** (quantity) and vitamin **adequacy** (quality). Not all sources of vitamins are adequate — even though they technically meet the requirements of a vitamin deficiency.

## Unfriendly Foods

Vegetables:

- *Cooked* beets, carrots, and corn
- Peas (shelled)

- Root vegetables (parsnips, turnips, rutabagas, celery root)
- Sweet potatoes
- Vegetable juices

"White" foods:

- Sugar and artificial sweeteners
- Cream, milk, mayonnaise, and creamy dressings
- Rice (including white and brown)
- Rice milk and soy milk
- Potatoes
- Pasta
- Flour
- Bread

"Beige" Foods:

- Bagels, pastries, and other bread products or breaded food
- Blended coffee drinks
- Cereals (hot and cold)
- Chips, crackers, cookies
- Deep-fried foods
- Pizza
- Tortillas (flour and corn)

Killer Fruits (calorie bombs):

- Dates
- Mangoes
- Pineapple
- Plantains
- Raisins
- *Ripe* bananas, papayas, and pears

- *Seedless* grapes
- Dried fruit and fruit strips
- Fruit juices

Other foods:

- Alcohol: mixed drinks, white and rose wine, beer, make liquors
- Honey, molasses, maple syrup, corn syrup, and other sweeteners
- Jan, jellies, preserves, and condiments made with sugar
- Soft drinks (including sugar-free and diet)

# Chapter 5: The First Two Weeks

Chapter 5 describes the first two weeks of Phase 1.

The Teardown Phase (Phase 1) is broken into an initial two-week period, followed by a slightly relaxed diet in the next four weeks. These first two weeks, however, involve more strictness on your food intake.

During this time, you're deactivating the "winter is coming" messages you've been sending to your genes (which trigger the "store fat for winter" program), and replacing them with messages that indicate "winter is now," which activates the burning of stored fat.

So how do you do it?

- One portion of protein (the size of your palm) for each meal (breakfast, lunch, and dinner).
- Plenty of leafy greens — you can eat as much as you want.
- Two snacks of seeds or nuts (1/4 cup each)
- 8-10 glasses of water
- NO fruits, and nothing from the "Unfriendly Foods" list in Ch. 4.

There are also some allowed treats:

- Red wine (women: 1 glass/day; men: 2 glasses/day)
- Spirits with no mixers (women: 1 shot/day; men: 2 shots/day)

Why does this regimen work during this part of the phase?

Digesting protein requires a lot of your body's energy —
the process of breaking it down into usable fuel requires
30% of the protein's calories, which means weight loss for
you.

The heat produced by the digestion of animal protein also
leads to a higher level of satiety. Which means you'll feel
more full.

Meanwhile, you can consume as many friendly vegetables
as you'd like. (*Note: unless you're already a big veggie
eater, you'll feel better if you gradually increase your
veggie consumption as your system adjusts to the new way
of eating.*)

In this stage, protein is providing most of your calories,
while vegetables are providing volume (to fill you up) and
micronutrients.

There are some early potential side effects to be aware
of...

You may get a headachey feeling for a few days in these
first two weeks as your body acclimates to burning fat for
energy.

You'll likely see an initial rapid loss of 3-5 pounds. This is a
result of your body releasing water that had been attached
to glycogen molecules (as part of your body's internal
distress system). For the same reason, you'll also feel less

bloated, and if you have high blood pressure, those levels may drop.

Although you're shedding pounds, you may see your body fat percentage increase (temporarily).

Gundry provides a few extra tips as you're going through this stage:

- Vary your veggies. This makes your meals more interesting and also gives you a more diverse intake of micronutrients. Additionally, your body is programmed to resist when you're eating too much of the same thing (in order to prevent your liver's detoxification system from becoming overloaded). So vary the types of greens and other veggies that you're taking in.
- Don't confuse high protein and high fat. Protein is the thing you're optimizing for, not fat.
- Use nuts and seeds to help you deal with cravings, so you can stay satisfied and motivated.

He also provides a few supplement recommendations:

- To help with sugar cravings, try selenium, cinnamon, and chromium.
- To promote gut health, try probiotics and prebiotics.

He closes with a reminder to do what you can, with what you've got, wherever you are. This applies not only any time you find yourself in a situation — say, at a dinner party or traveling — where you can't stick to the regimen exactly. It also is an important thing to remember as you try to make any dramatic changes. Go gradually as you move away from the tastes you've become accustomed to and switch to new ones. The purpose is to find longevity, which means this is a long game — don't try to rush it.

# Chapter 6: What's Off the Menu?

Chapter 6 provides support as you move through the first two weeks.

Gundry opens with a reminder that the purpose of this phase is to convince your genetic programming that winter is not coming — that winter is here — in order to stop your genes from sending the message that your body needs to store fat for winter.

This means that some of the foods you're avoiding in this stage (including fruit) are good for you — they're just not good for this stage. They're counterproductive to the new signals you need to initiate in your genetic communications system because they activate the "store fat for winter" program.

As you make changes, you'll break your (actually, your body's) addiction to the old foods it thought it needed.

He gives another reminder that as you move along, you should do so gradually. For example, if you're habituated to sweet tastes, try starting out by using fewer sweeteners. Gundry recommends a strategy called "pinch the packet" — meaning that if you're accustomed to using an entire packet of sweetener in your coffee, for example, pinch the packet and use only half of it. Then tomorrow, use only 1/4 of the packet until you've weaned yourself off completely.

With regard to weight loss, he also makes a few points:

First, weight loss is not like clockwork. Stick to the program, and over time, you'll see the pounds add up.

Also, thin people on a poor diet often experience the same health problems associated with killer gene activation as those who are overweight. While the focus of this phase is on weight loss, the ultimate goal is health — and you're making those healthy changes, regardless of how quickly you can see them taking effect.

Furthermore, with the exception of the first two weeks, it's always a good idea to lose weight slowly. Why? Because we, like all animals, store heavy metals (like lead and mercury, and other toxins) in our fat cells. As fat is burned, those toxins are released into our bloodstream. This can be safely flushed out of your system when you slowly shed the weight — but if you go too quickly, it can be lethal. **A rate of 50 pounds lost per year (roughly one per week) is a safe place.**

Gundry provides some additional tips as you navigate these two weeks:

- In general, if a package says "all-natural," "fat-free," "no cholesterol," "heart-healthy," "sugar-free," "no added sugar," or the like, run the other way.
- Milk contains IGF, which acts like insulin in your liver and triggers the "store fat for the winter program." Skim milk contains even more sugar than whole milk. Stay away.

He also makes some new supplement recommendations. These, he refers to as the "Fab Five:"

- Vitamin E — *make sure it's "mixed vitamin E" or includes d-alpha tocopherols (not dl)*
- Vitamin C
- Magnesium
- Folic Acid
- Other B Vitamins

**Measuring Your Progress**

Gundry states that it's normal to lose at least three pounds in this stage, although he's seen results range from two pounds to as much as 12 pounds in this two-week period.

If you're not losing weight, however, it's time to start a food diary and write down *everything* that goes into your mouth. Gundry says it usually only takes a few days of doing this before it becomes obvious where you're accidentally consuming something you shouldn't be.

Note that young women are likely to lose weight more slowly than men (because women store body fat for reproduction and nursing).

When you've reached the end of the two weeks, it's time to decide for yourself whether to move on or if you should remain here for a few more weeks. Ask yourself:

- How much weight did you want to lose? (Recommended: stay in this phase until you've reached a BMI of 29.)
- Do you have diabetes or metabolic syndrome? (Recommended: stay in this phase until your sugar and insulin levels normalize.)

## Chapter 7: The Teardown Continues

This chapter walks you through the remainder of Phase 1 (the last four weeks).

As you're progressing through Phase 1, your genes are getting the message loud and clear: there are no trees full of sugary fruit around to feast on, and most of your calories come from protein, so it must be the depths of winter. And because you're getting plenty of protein, as well as carbohydrates in all those veggies, your genes are reassured that you're not in starvation mode.

For the remainder of the Teardown (the next four weeks), you should continue to avoid "beige" and "white" foods (from the "Unfriendly Foods" list in Ch. 4) to the best of your ability. You can also make the following changes:

1.  Add back in black, blue, and red fruits. These are full of phytonutrients, which can help turn on your longevity genes, improve brain function, and turn off killer genes.
2.  Add up to two servings per day of apples and citrus fruits, as well as tomatoes and avocados. (But continue to steer clear of the "Killer Fruits" listed in Ch. 4.)
3.  Add up to 1/2 cup per day of cooked *whole* grains or legumes. Gundry refers to these as "brown" foods. Note that this slight relaxation on whole grains does not extend to bread or to anything else on the "white" and "beige" lists (Ch. 4).

All of these additions are optional. If you'd like to continue without any of them, feel free to do so. Note that adding these items back into your diet may slow down weight loss.

Finally, there's one more chance to make as you continue through this phase: you should gradually decrease the size of your protein portions and simultaneously increase your leafy greens and other "friendly vegetable" (i.e. nothing on the "Unfriendly" list) intake. In doing so, you're decreasing the amount of calorie-dense but micronutrient-sparse food and increasing foods denser in micronutrients and lower in calories.

By the end of the sixth week, your protein portions should be half the size of your palm.

If you're struggling with letting go of "white" and "beige" foods, Gundry suggests following...

**Pasta**: If you're someone who really loves pasta, he recommends what he calls "Fool-dles," a pseudo-pasta made using tofu shirataki noodles, found in the refrigerated section of Trader Joe's, Whole Foods, and some grocery stores.

**Oatmeal**: "Old fashioned," "rolled," or "quick" oats have all been stripped of their nutritive properties and are instantly digested into sugar. Steel-cut, Scottish, or Irish oats fall closer to the whole grain category and may be considered "brown" foods.

It's notable that most cultures that incorporate white and beige foods as an energy source without apparent ill effect have found ways of dealing with the glycemic impact of these foods and regularly expend large amounts of energy (such as 14-hour days of manual labor in a rice paddy).

Unless you plan on mimicking their entire lifestyle, don't use these populations as an excuse to keep eating anything on the white or beige lists.

Gundry also gives a few notes on "brown" foods...

**Whole grains**: A truly whole grain may be safe to eat — but it comes at a price if weight loss is your goal, thanks to its dense concentration of calories.

**Legumes**: These are also dense in calories, largely from sugars. Approach legumes with a similar attitude as you have toward whole grains.

If you're still not convinced, consider the following: If you want to fatten up a cow or chicken, feed them grains. Any questions?

To help you understand more about what's happening when you eat certain foods, Gundry summarizes what's happening in this stage with **cholesterol**, **triglycerides**, and **fats and oils**:

### Cholesterol

You may be familiar with "good" cholesterol (HDL) and "bad" cholesterol (LDL). What you may not know is there are seven kinds of LDL — three dangerous and four friendly. And there are five kinds of HDL — but only one of those five is doing the heavy lifting in cleaning your arteries.

Gundry writes, "Despite what you've been told about how important your genes are in determining your risk of high cholesterol, and in how trans fats elevate your LDL, my research has demonstrated that the sugar and starches in the food you eat almost completely determine your cholesterol levels and the ratio of good to bad cholesterol."

Additionally, approx. 25% of us carry a gene that codes for what Gundry calls "bad cholesterol with an attitude" — Lipoprotein(a), or Lp(a). If you find Lp(a) in your system, the supplements CoQ10 and niacin (Vitamin B3) should help your levels normalize.

## Triglycerides

A person's triglyceride level corresponds exactly to the amount of white, beige, and brown foods they're consuming, as well as fruit intake (especially the "killer fruits").

If your triglycerides fall, you'll lose weight and your LDL levels will drop. And unlike other diet programs, the weight stays off when you follow Diet Evolution, because here you've also inactivated the "store fat for winter" program.

## Fats and Oils

There are naturally occurring fats, and there are manufactured fats.

Manufactured fats (known as trans fats) appear on labels as hydrogenated or partially hydrogenated oils and should be avoided as much as possible. These are used in processed or fast foods to keep them from spoiling. They're associated with higher levels of LDL.

Animal fats are completely different in today's world than they were 100 years ago, thanks to the grain-based diet we now feed them.

When animals — especially fish — consume plants, they absorb whatever fats were contained in the plants' leaves. Algae, seaweed, and krill are rich in omega-3 oils, which become concentrated in the fat stores of the fish that feed on them and get passed along the food chain to us. Gundry refers to this as "green" oil, since it provides the most omega-3 value.

Other "green" oils include:

- Fish oil
- Extra virgin olive oil
- Avocado oil
- Purslane (a common weed)
- Perilla oil

There are also what Gundry calls "brown" oils — fats high in the omega-3 fatty acid alpha-linolenic acid (ALA).

"Brown" oils can be derived from:

- Walnuts
- Flaxseed
- Rapeseed
- Hemp seed

"Green" and "brown" oils are contrasted with "beige" grain-based oils (such as corn, soybean, cottonseed, safflower). Green and brown oils are rich in omega-3s, while beige oils are high in omega-6s. The modern diet tilts too heavily toward omega-6s (refer to Ch. 2), and it's important to restore the 1:1 ratio between the two.

This imbalance means you're overproducing pain and inflammation hormones and under-producing pain-relieving, anti-inflammatory hormones. By switching to a higher intake of green and brown oils, you're beginning to correct these hormone levels.

Restoring this 1:1 ratio accomplishes something else: it curbs cravings for sweet foods (win-win!)

Gundry gives some extra tips on using oils:

- Do not cook with flaxseed or hemp oil (because cooking oxidizes them).
- Store flaxseed and hemp oils in the refrigerator.
- Buy olive, fish, flaxseed, and hemp oils in dark containers to prevent them from going rancid.
- If you buy fish oil supplements, look for capsules or bottled oil that is "molecularly distilled" (meaning that the heavy metals that concentrate on fish fat have been removed).

Furthermore, as you're buying foods, keep the following in mind:

The more the original food has been altered, the less you should eat it.

The more you extend a food's shelf life, the more it shortens your life.

Supplement recommendations given at this stage include:

- For hypertension, try anything containing hawthorn berries, olive leaf extract, magnesium, and manganese, which help dilate (relax) blood vessels.
- As immune function and athletic performance enhancers, try cranberry extract, grape skin extract, grape seed extract, pycnogenols, or mushroom extracts (especially reishi, cordyceps, or maitake).

# Chapter 8: Settling In

This chapter discusses some progress markers you can watch for, as well as what to do when you hit the inevitable plateau.

Aside from weight loss, here's what you should expect to be experiencing at this point:

- If you have a history of aching joints or other aches and pains, you should be feeling better.
- Headaches may be less frequent and less intense.
- Heartburn should have subsided or vanished.
- If you're on hypertension meds, you may get an occasional dizzy spell because your blood pressure is normalizing and your dosage needs to be adjusted.
- If you take diabetes pills or insulin shots, you also may experience occasional dizziness as your blood sugar level drops naturally, indicating your prescription also needs to be adjusted.
- Life's pleasures may be coming into sharper focus as your body stops firing off pain signals and begins sending out more pleasure signals. (And when you feel this sense of renewal, don't be surprised if you find you're suddenly inclined to rearrange your bookcases, give a dinner party, or pick up that tennis racket. These activities, in turn, prompt your genes to send out even more pleasure signals.)

Six weeks into the diet is a good point to check in with your physician and get re-tested on the same markers you began with. When you do, you should see:

- Total cholesterol down by ~50 points.
- Lower LDL
- Higher HDL
- Triglyceride level down
- Insulin level down
- Blood glucose level down
- Blood pressure down
- Body fat percentage down

If this is what you see, then it's evidence that the "store fat for winter" program has been deactivated. You're sending new signals to your genes, and they're responding.

**The Plateau**

When it comes to the weight loss you may be experiencing, there's an important point to be aware of: at some point in the first phase (anywhere from 4-12 weeks in), you will hit a plateau.

A plateau is when you've gone two or more weeks without any weight loss. What's happening here? Gundry writes:

"Relax. You've just hit the first of many readjustment spots. I have come to welcome these spots, as much as I welcome a readjustment phase in a yoga pose."

He points out that if you examine any training regimen, the introduction of mandatory rest periods inevitably improves performance.

When you're in the plateau stage, welcome it. Treat it as an opportunity to "settle in" to this new place.

So why does this plateau happen? Because you've lost the fat cells that used to "eat" the food you were consuming. (In order to exist for 24 hours, each pound of cells uses about 10 calories.)

Your new goal (for the time being) is just to keep your weight stable. After your body adjusts, weight loss should resume again. This is also an opportunity to learn what it takes to hold yourself at a lower weight.

It's not problematic if you plateau — it's problematic if you *don't* plateau. Embrace it instead of resisting or trying to force your way out of it. Settle in, and let your body adjust in the way it needs to as you continue your journey into health and longevity.

Gundry closes with one more reason to embrace a slower weight loss pace: If you lose weight slowly, your skin will keep up with it. If you lose weight too fast, you'll almost always need plastic surgery to get rid of excess skin.

**What if you're gaining weight?**

Gundry writes, "If your weight starts to rise, I can virtually guarantee you that sugary [foods] or foods that quickly turn into sugar are creeping back into your diet. Look carefully at what you're eating and you'll find them." Begin keeping a food diary and write down every single thing that goes into your mouth for two weeks. Examine for common culprits Gundry refers to as the "Dirty Dozen."

The Dirty Dozen:

- "No sugar added" jams, pies, and juices
- High-protein energy bars (sports bars, energy bars, or diet bars)
- Trail mix or granola
- Fruit-filled breakfast bars or flavored yogurts
- Canned vegetable or fruit juices
- Flavored water or sports drinks
- Diet soft drinks
- Lattes or frappuccinos with skim milk or soy milk
- "Whole grain" cereals, crackers, or bread
- Foods labeled "low fat," "fat-free," "no sugar," or "no cholesterol"
- Anything containing sugar under one of its aliases: cane sugar, natural sugar, date sugar, organic sugar, or various syrups.
- Too many nuts. Just how big is that handful of nuts you're snacking on? Make sure it's no more than 1/4 cup.

If the plateau lasts more than two weeks and you're not falling on one of the Dirty Dozen, you're eating too much protein. Halve your portions, and weight loss should resume.

**Handling Cravings**

There are some other things you can expect at this point in the process...

Research indicates that this plateau period is characterized by a huge increase in the hunger-stimulating hormone ghrelin, which actually makes you fantasize about food, especially sugars and starches. This is especially true in the summer months when ghrelin levels are already at their highest — your body's way of getting you to stock up on fruits so you can store fat for winter.

By **continuing to stick to the program**, you're telling your genes that you're ok — you're not starving to death, and winter is not coming.

There's another thing you can do to combat this hormone's message: sleep more. The two hormones responsible for controlling hunger and satiety, ghrelin and leptin (respectively), are very sensitive to light and sleep duration. Sleeping longer raises your leptin (satiety) levels and lowers ghrelin (hunger) levels.

There's evidence that a number of Western diseases didn't exist before electricity became prevalent, messing with our circadian rhythms. When you're sleeping longer, your genes interpret that to mean that winter is here and it's time to stop storing fat and start burning it in order to keep you alive.

An extra bonus is that when you're sleeping, you can't be eating.

Additionally, as discussed in Ch. 7, you can increase your omega-3 intake by using more green and brown oils on your meals. As your omega-3 and omega-6 levels rebalance, you should feel fewer sugar cravings.

Gundry also makes some supplement suggestions to help stave off hunger cravings:

- St. John's Wort (also works as a mood elevator and antidepressant)
- SAM-e (also works as a mood elevator and provides benefits to joint and liver function)
- Citromax, aka garcinia cambazola

**Exercise**

Increasing muscle mass can actually interfere with weight loss goals because muscle weighs more than the fat it displaces — so you shouldn't expect exercise to speed up your progress in these first weeks. (When exercising, your clothes will fit better, however — so you may see it in your jeans before you see it on the scale.)

While weight loss isn't a substantial side effect of exercise, incorporating more movement into your day should lead to a number of positive psychological effects. (But keep it mild to moderate, unless you're accustomed to high-intensity workouts. More on this in the next chapter.) Gundry recommends yoga or tai chi as mechanisms by which you can begin to flood your brain with more pleasure signals. But you can find whatever outlet is most enjoyable for you.

**Moving onto Phase 2**

Have you lost all the pounds you wanted to lose or do you continue to drop a pound per week? If so, great — you've successfully activated the "winter is now" program, and you're burning fat for energy

If you'd like to lose more weight, it's your decision whether to remain in Phase 1 for a little while longer or to move onto Phase 2.

If you have health issues, be sure to see your physician before moving onto Phase 2. Specifically, you should have the following checked:

- Is your insulin resistance gone or nearly gone? If not, stay in Teardown until you've lost at least 20 pounds.
- Has your LDL cholesterol level increased? If so, you're part of a small group of people who have this response to a high-protein, higher animal fat diet. Time to start rebuilding by moving to the Restoration phase.

# Chapter 9: Begin the Restoration

Chapter 9 introduces Phase 2 of the program.

During this phase (which you should follow for a minimum of six weeks), you'll gradually advance toward deriving most of your protein from vegetables, nuts, and eggs. As you eat more vegetables, your body will adjust to their high micronutrients and phytochemical content. Continue to eat your nut or seed snack twice/day and steer clear of "white" and "beige" foods. Eat whole grains and legumes in extreme moderation (no more than 1/2 cup cooked) or not at all.

The foods you're eating in Phase 2 are basically the same as Phase 1, except you're now eating more of some and less of others. You're decreasing the density of your food and increasing the volume of calorie-sparse foods so that it speeds through your system, turns off the hunger switch, and lowers your metabolism. This means gradually eating less meat, poultry, fish, and cheese, and fewer grains and legumes.

The animal protein, which was an integral part of the wrecking crew during Teardown, is, unfortunately, going to start turning on you if you don't make a switch. (This is one reason why high-fat, high-protein programs don't work in the long-term.)

Do a mind flip: It's time to start seeing vegetables as the main dish and animal protein as the side.

Rather than think you need to become vegetarian or vegan, Gundry suggests a new term: "Vegephile," one who likes to eat vegetables.

If you're following the reverse-evolutionary timeline, here's where we are:

- In Phase 1, you followed a way of eating that was as close as possible to the way people ate roughly a century ago.
- During the next six or more weeks (Phase 2), you'll evolve your eating patterns to mimic the diet of our ancestors before the onset of agriculture and domestication of animals occurred, roughly 10,000 years ago.

**Why reduce animal protein?**

How is it that eating lots of animal protein becomes harmful in the long-term? Because the process of breaking down proteins from anything with flesh generates heat.

To your genetic autopilot, this heat indicates that you're terribly inefficient at burning fuel and that you're working much harder than you should be. It indicates that you're like a car getting 10 miles to the gallon.

If you've ever found brown liver spots on your skin (AGE spots), that's your body's warning sign that you're generating too much heat.

As you make the shift during Phase 2, you're sending a new message to your genes: That you are not a threat to future generations, because you're not gobbling up more than your fair share of food.

**Can veggies effectively replace animal protein?**

Animals that eat only green growing things don't get fat, develop heart disease, or become diabetic. Humans who follow a raw and living food diet often have trouble gaining weight. Why? In part, it's because the micronutrients and the bulk of plant fiber activate the ultimate satiation hormones produced by cells in your lower digestive tract, turning on your "I'm not hungry" hormone switch.

The faster food moves through your lower bowel, the more anti-hunger hormones in your intestinal cells beam up to your brain.

Additionally, you can eat a higher volume of greens without the negative effects of eating that same volume of animal products, grains, or legumes. For example, a one-inch cube of cheese contains up to 250 calories (almost all fat, with a little protein). Meanwhile, it would take eating five to eight bags of romaine to reach the same number of calories — plus the romaine is packed with huge quantities of phytonutrients.

What about protein? Can you get enough protein just from veggies?

Think of gorillas and chimps: A 400-pound male silverback gorilla consumes 16 pounds of leaves a day, but only 3% of his body composition is fat. He's pure muscle mass, all generated from the protein in leaves.

It turns out that there's actually more protein contained in 100 calories of broccoli than there is in 100 calories of filet mignon. So, yes, by consuming more greens and fewer animal products, you can continue to meet your body's protein requirements.

One last note on this:

In Phase 1, you learned that consuming animal products from animals that consumed green things was beneficial. That was true, but it was because animals were the middleman between green things and you. As you move through this phase of the program, you cut out the middleman to deliver the best stuff directly into your system.

If you can work your way up to consuming the equivalent of one bag of dark green leaves (lettuce, spinach, or other greens) daily, your life will change dramatically for the better.

**Clearing up the confusion on calories**

"Calorie-sparse" is not the same as "low calorie."

The vegetables you're eating more of are calorie-sparse, not because they don't contain calories, but because their calories aren't all digested and absorbed as calories. (For example, half of the carbohydrates in romaine lettuce take the form of water-soluble fiber.) Therefore, the calories in greens don't activate the "store fat for winter" program.

In closing, Gundry writes, "Studies show that despite living longer, we're experiencing deterioration in the quality of our health. Surviving is not synonymous with thriving."

The key to the Restoration phase is the transition from calorie-dense foods to calorie-sparse foods. This results not only in long-term weight control but also in long-term *thriving health*.

# Chapter 10: Picking Up the Pace

This chapter is all about exercise.

Just as our eating habits have changed over time, so too have our patterns of movement and natural exercise. But all research on successful long-term weight loss indicates that some form of exercise program is essential to maintaining a lowered weight.

At some point, you'll reach a tipping point in your food intake, where you're no longer willing to reduce the number of calories you're taking in. Once you've reached that mile marker, any additional calories that you want to consume will need to be earned with physical labor if you don't want them stored as fat.

Building muscle mass has another benefit: lower insulin levels. (Why? Because as you build muscle mass, the insulin that's circulating in your body is able to do its job delivering energy to those muscles. This prevents your pancreas from producing higher levels of insulin in an effort to push food into cells that it assumes are blocked with fat.)

Lowering insulin levels keeps your "store fat for winter" program turned off and, more importantly, prevents insulin from stimulating the growth of cells that don't need stimulating (i.e. cancer).

An important note to keep in mind when choosing a movement or exercise plan is to pick something that you can develop into a habit. Otherwise, it won't stick, and you'll be left frustrated.

On the topic of exercise, Gundry discusses both running/walking and strength training:

**Running and Walking**

Animals move for only two reasons: to find food or to keep from being someone else's food.

These behaviors align with research findings on health in runners: people who go long distances at a slow and steady pace exhibit more optimal health than those who do long distances at a fast pace. Sprinters also exhibit optimal health as a result of their practice of going short distances as fast as they can.

This leads to the conclusion: If you're doing a *distance* run or walk, slow down your pace. If you're doing a *short* distance, push your speed as fast as you can.

Another hack when going long distances: If you do a long walk *after* a meal, you'll drop more pounds than if you do that same walk before the meal. Why? Because your body doesn't know if you'll be walking for one mile or for twenty. So it doesn't make sense to store the food you just ate as fat, since you may need all those calories on your trek.

## Strength Training

In the past, both men and women collected food — whether prey, leaves, berries, or tubers — and carried it back to a central camp. Today, we call this type of movement strength training.

By developing a weight lifting practice, you communicate to your genes that you're a contributing member of the tribe and that you should be kept around as someone who's useful to the continuation of the species.

Our ancestors lifted, pulled, wrestled, and sprinted after things; they also walked long distances. The more you duplicate these actions, the more your genes will identify your behavior as a successful animal.

As you seek to develop your own exercise habits, Gundry suggests the following resources:

- The Power of Ten, by Adam Zickerman
- The Slow Burn Fitness Revolution, by Fredrick Hahn

He also makes the following supplements recommendations:

- CoQ10: helps with muscle pains or weakness and congestive heart failure
- Acetyl-L-carnitine or L-carnitine: helps strengthen muscle tissue; great for people with a history of congestive heart failure and cardiomyopathy

## Moving onto Phase 3

After you've spent at least six weeks in Phase 2 — assuming you're getting close to your goal weight and your cholesterol and other markers indicate you're continuing to make progress — it's time to think about moving to Phase 3. If you're happy spending more time in this phase, however, continue to do so until you're ready to move on.

# Chapter 11: Thriving for a Good, Long Time

Chapter 11 introduces the third and final phase of the Diet Evolution program.

Time for Phase 3 — the Longevity Phase.

Up until now, you've been eating both cooked and raw foods. In Phase 3, you move to eat primarily raw food, as our earliest ancestors did.

Eating food raw generally preserves more of the micronutrients (although there are exceptions to this).

Another benefit to raw food is that it is considerably bulkier than its cooked counterpart. All that raw bulk makes you feel satisfyingly full, so you eat fewer calories.

Before moving on, Gundry gives a reminder: Do what you can, with what you have, wherever you are. None of the parameters of Phase 3 are written law — they're merely suggestions, information, and options, with which you can make your own decisions about how to live your life.

## Why Raw?

First, it's important to understand **hormesis** — what it is and the role it plays here.

Hormesis is the favorable response of an organism to low exposures of toxins and other stressors (which, in larger doses, would cause a negative response). This is what

Gundry is referring to when he says that the things that are "bad" for you are actually good for you. Hormesis is critical in activating your body's longevity program: a little stress goes a long way.

All plants and animals possess subtle sensors that alert genes of approaching hard times so they can take measures to protect themselves. The key to your longevity program is the self-protective response that kicks in when scarcity threatens.

Hormesis improves resistance to infections, tumors, and even death.

All research on hormesis in humans suggests that there's a point in every exposure to a stressor or toxin that instigates not only survival but thriving.

When your genes sense too much stress, they conclude that you're not a successful animal and therefore don't need to be protected and preserved, and your killer genes are activated. But at the right dose, these same potentially lethal stimuli promote and maximize health.

**Moderate exercise** is one known hormetic stressor that increases lifespan (though too much exercise stress can shorten lifespan, in keeping with the hormetic curve).

**Calorie optimization** is another one. Eating just enough calories (while getting plenty of micronutrients) extends lifespan by as much as 600% in some species. No matter what type of food they eat, animals that consume fewer calories live longer. Calorie optimization is the practice you've been developing all along in this program.

All vegetables have hormetic properties, but **bitter vegetables** are the strongest. Populations that favor bitter foods (like the Japanese and Italians) are noted for both longevity and short stature.

**Plant toxins** also induce hormesis. But many plant toxins are reduced or inactivated when they're cooked — and this is the reason why, in Phase 3, you transition to a more raw diet. How much is enough? Gundry writes, "My successful patient volunteers, meaning those who permanently change their body and blood chemistry, do so by evolving to a diet that is at least 60% raw food."

Note that raw foods should be added to your diet slowly to avoid experiencing any toxic responses such as headaches, rashes, diarrhea, and joint aches.

Finally, **fasting** is another behavior that can cause hormesis. (More on this in the next chapter.)

# Chapter 12: Tricking Your Genes: Beyond Diet

Chapter 12 dives more deeply into opportunities for creating hormetic stressors before closing out with some last notes and a final farewell as you continue your life-long journey.

At this point, you've been following many practices of calorie optimization, and you've begun applying the principles of hormesis to your lifestyle. In this chapter, Gundry shares more ways to create hormetic responses that benefit your health.

As a caveat, he writes that for each of the following, "You may be inclined to go all the way with me, you may decide none of these ideas are for you, or you may wind up somewhere in the middle." Each is merely a suggestion, not a requirement.

**Fasting**

You can capitalize on the hormetic properties of fasting by doing any of the following:

- Fast every other day and eat two days' worth of food on alternate days. (This may be done once/week or as an ongoing pattern.)
- Skip a meal. (Start with one day/week, then perhaps increase the frequency.)

- Eat only one meal/day, getting all of your calories in that one meal.

There are, however, some important notes to keep in mind about fasting:

- Be realistic. Evolve your habits slowly over time — don't try to jump in the deep end right at the start.
- Don't abuse these tools in order to lose weight. The purpose is health and longevity.

## Alcohol

The toxin ethanol can be found in all forms of alcohol and is another hormetic stressor. Consuming small quantities per day — 1-2 servings for women; 2-3 servings for men — has been shown to lead to longer life and lower rates of heart disease. In small doses, alcohol stimulates the manufacturing of TPA and nitric oxide, which both works to open up your blood vessels.

Red wine can be particularly beneficial, thanks to a phytochemical called resveratrol, found in red grapes. Resveratrol stimulates your anti-aging genes and is preserved in the fermentation process used for red wine

This one comes with another important proviso: Alcohol carries a steep risk-to-benefit ratio. If you don't currently drink alcohol or have a history of alcoholism, there's no need to integrate this into your new lifestyle. Alcohol is powerful — don't mess with it if there's any chance it might win.

## Coffee, Tea, & Chocolate

All three of these products also stimulate a hormetic response.

The phytochemical EGCG in cocoa seems to act much like plant toxins in its effect on your body.

In coffee and tea, bitter polyphenols stimulate low levels of stress. (Just be sure not to drink more than five cups a day — five cups are the hormetic tipping point.)

It's important to note, however, that the active ingredients in each of these products are completely inactivated by milk. So when it comes to chocolate, stick only to very dark (with a cocoa content of 70% or higher), and leave milk out of your beverages.

It's also worth noting that the benefits of coffee and tea are only released in the presence of caffeine. So unless you have an issue with heart palpitations, stay away from decaf.

## Temperature

Exposure to higher than normal body temperatures for even short periods of time activates the production of compounds known as heat-shock proteins, which go around telling any cell that isn't pulling its weight to self-destruct — leaving only fresh, healthy cells.

Similarly, a compound that activates cell protectors has been found to be triggered by extreme cold.

Exposing yourself to both extremes in temperature signals your genes to take up a defensive posture.

## Supplements

At a certain dose, almost all vitamins, minerals, and other supplements show toxic side effects. It seems that they follow the exact same hormetic curve we've been discussing.

Keep this in mind as you begin integrating supplements into your diet — more of a good thing isn't always a good thing. Don't overdo it. After a certain point, these same supplements that are "good" for you will become bad for you.

## Breaking from the diet

Once you've deactivated the "store fat for winter" program, it's fine to take a break from the diet occasionally. You've normalized your lipid and glucose levels, and the occasional cheat day won't have any ill effects on your health. (Just don't let it turn into a habit!)

**As long as the overall trend of your diet and lifestyle challenges your body with low-level stressors, your**

**health, your resistance to infection, and your vitality will improve. And as long as you're consuming the optimal number of calories, you won't regain the weight.**

**It's Never Too Late**

Working with patients in their 80s and beyond, Gundry closes the book with this emphasis: It's never too late to give yourself a new life. It takes only 90 days for your cells to become almost fully rewritten. You can still make the most of whatever years you have remaining and find new rejuvenation and vibrancy. ...You may even be surprised by how much is still available to you, even now.

Gundry closes with a final well-wish:

Live long and prosper.

# Background on *Dr. Gundry's Diet Evolution*

While Gundry's career has always been in the medical field, he himself had never been a picture of health. Obese, with poor cholesterol and blood pressure levels, skin tags, and frequent migraines — none of the workouts, diets, or other "healthy" changes he tried made any difference for him.

Then one day in 2001, a man who Gundry refers to as "Big Ed" strode into his office.

Big Ed had been diagnosed with cholesterol plaques and blockages in his arteries so severe they were inoperable. Even Gundry, who has a history of performing on impossible cases, agreed that Big Ed was beyond operation. Big Ed then told Gundry that since his last angiogram, he'd lost 45 pounds and had been taking handfuls of herbs and supplements daily. Gundry's response was a typical one — that those supplements made only "expensive urine" and wouldn't make a difference — but Big Ed convinced him to perform a new angiogram anyway.

To his surprise, the second angiogram revealed that Big Ed's blockages had shrunk by more than 50%. And, while his arteries were still very diseased, an operation was now feasible.

Following Big Ed's quintuple bypass later that week, Gundry asked him to bring in his vitamins, minerals, and herbs and to share how he had constructed his diet. As he listened, he was transported back to his university research involving human evolutionary biology. Thus begun Gundry's personal quest to understand the natural workings that underpin human health.

Over the course of that year, everything changed for Gundry — or, better yet, he changed everything. He modified his own diet based on the evolutionary genetic coding that he had previously studied and reversed all of his medical problems. As his health improved, he also dropped 75 pounds.

He began applying these principles in his consultations with patients and consistently saw similar results.

This moved him to walk away from his professorship and to open his own institute, where he now trains anyone who wants to improve their health in the methods of the Diet Evolution.

# Author Background

## Education and Philosophy

In school, Gundry's interest was in Human Evolutionary Biology — an interest that has informed all of his medical work, but that has become particularly relevant in his current work with the Diet Evolution program.

He completed his undergrad degree in the Honors program at Yale University, graduated Alpha Omega Alpha from the Medical College of Georgia School of Medicine, completed residencies in General Surgery and Thoracic Surgery at the University of Michigan, and served as a Clinical Associate at the National Institutes of Health.

At the NIH, he developed methods and treatments to prevent and reverse damage in coronary arteries and heart muscle cells — a precursor to his later inventions.

## Accomplishments and Accolades

Until 2001, most of Gundry's work was as a surgeon and as a researcher on how to keep heart cells alive under stress.

Following his career launch in the NIH, he completed a fellowship in congenital heart surgery at The Hospital for Sick Children in London and served as a professor for two years at the University of Maryland School of Medicine

Working as a surgeon, he invented the Gundry Retrograde Cardioplegia Cannula, one of the most widely-used devices to keep the heart muscle alive during open-heart surgery. The effectiveness of this device surprised many: before it was developed, most surgeons were trying to push important heart-protective ingredients "forward" into the heart — but Gundry hypothesized that by pushing those same ingredients "backward," it would be more effective, and he was right. His idea was rejected and laughed at by many accredited surgeons, but today, it's the gold standard in protecting the heart during surgery.

Gundry also holds patents on a number of other devices used to repair leaky heart valves or to "sew" new blood vessels into the heart without sutures. He and his colleague Leonard Bailey have together performed more infant and pediatric heart transplants than anyone else in the world. His lab also holds the record for producing the longest surviving pig-to-baboon heart transplant. He was also one of the first of twenty to test the first successful artificial heart, one of the first to use robots in operation, and the very first to design and perform heart-valve operations through two-inch holes.

His other accolades and achievements could go on for pages — here are some of the highlights:

- 16 years as a professor of Surgery and Pediatrics in Cardiothoracic Surgery, Loma Linda School of Medicine

- Former Chairman and Head of Cardiothoracic Surgery, Loma Linda School of Medicine
- Current Fellow of the American Surgical Association, the American College of Surgeons, the American College of Cardiology, the American Academy of Pediatrics, and the College of Chest Physicians.
- Has repeatedly been elected as a Castle Connelly Top American Doctor
- Has published 300+ articles, abstracts, and book chapters
- The inventor of the Gundry Ministernotomy (the most widely used minimally invasive technique for operating on the aortic or mitral valves)
- The inventor of the Gundry Lateral Tunnel (a "living" tissue that can rebuild parts of the heart in children with severe congenital heart malformations)
- The inventor of the Skoosh venous cannula (the most widely used cannula in minimally invasive heart operations)

He also consulted for the film *The Doctor* — starring William Hurt, about a heart surgeon diagnosed with a life-threatening disease and decides to change his ways — and performed a bit part in the movie.

He lives with his family in Palm Springs, California.

**The International Heart and Lung Institute**

Upon recognizing the power of proper diet and lifestyle choices on health and longevity, Gundry left his post at Loma Linda University to open The International Heart and Lung Institute. There, he began offering the Diet Evolution program to former heart surgery patients as a restorative method. Before long, however, others began showing up, looking for help in their weight loss and health.

He continues to practice surgery part-time, but most of his days are devoted to training and supporting people in the methods of the Diet Evolution.

### No More Mr. Knife-Guy

Gundry's purpose is now to teach patients how to stay away from him, which has earned him the nickname "No More Mr. Knife-Guy."

## Gundryisms

Dr. Gundry shares what his patients have begun to call "Gundryisms" — simple phrases to help you remember important concepts.

- Halt if you taste salt. (refer to Ch. 2)
- When in doubt, leave it out. (refer to Ch. 4)
- Retreat from sweet. (refer to Ch. 4)
- If it's "white," keep it out of sight. If it's "beige," better behave. If it's "brown," slow down. (refer to Ch. 4)
- [During Phase 1] You get to cheat if you eat protein or meat. (refer to Ch. 5)
- You just can't beat one pound per week! (refer to Ch. 6)
- If you eat fake fats, you get heart attacks! (refer to Ch. 7)
- Eat "green" or "brown" oil, and your belly fat will recoil. (refer to Ch. 7)
- If it's green, you'll grow lean. (refer to Ch. 7)
- Give fruit the boot. (refer to Ch. 7)
- Weight off fast will never last; weight off slow, you're good to go! (refer to Ch. 7)
- If you eat meat, you'll generate heat. (refer to Ch. 9)
- [During Phase 2] If you want to stick around, cut back on brown. (refer to Ch. 9)
- To earn it, you must burn it. (refer to Ch. 10)
- If you lift weights, you'll lose weight. (refer to Ch. 10)
- If you cut down on meat, you'll reduce your heat. (refer to Ch. 10)

- A lot of greens plus a bit of meat make a meal that can't be beaten. (refer to Ch. 10)
- If you eat dark green, you'll become lean. (refer to Ch. 10)
- The more you eat greens, the better you'll fit into those jeans! (refer to Ch. 10)
- If you run long, go slow; if you run short, go fast. (refer to Ch. 10)
- Sprint fast, and you'll build muscle mass. (refer to Ch. 10)
- More bitter, more better. (refer to Ch. 11)
- If you drink red wine, you'll be fine! (refer to Ch. 12)
- If you eat less, you'll live longer. (refer to Ch. 12)
- Eat food "live" [raw] to arrive at a hundred and five. (refer to Ch. 12)
- Vegetables are good for you because they're "bad" for you. (refer to Ch. 12)
- Keep your genes guessing as to the timing of your next meal [by fasting]. (refer to Ch. 12)

# Program Guide

You can use this section as a reference as you walk through the Diet Evolution program.

## Tracking Your Progress

Track your progress using the following indicators. Start by getting a baseline test, and monitor your levels as you go along.

- blood pressure
- heart rate
- fasting glucose level
- hemoglobin A1C
- fasting insulin level
- fasting lipid panel (preferably with fractions of LDL, HDL, Lp(a), Apo B, and Lipo-PLA2)
- homocysteine
- fibrinogen
- C-reactive protein (CRP)
- body fat percentage

*Important Note: You should move slowly through the program. Pushing through too quickly can be dangerous and counterproductive. Additionally, if you're on medications (particularly for hypertension or diabetes), be sure to check in with your physician regularly so your dosages can be modified as your natural levels normalize.

**Phase 1: The Teardown**

Purpose: weight loss

Duration: minimum 6 weeks, or until you're satisfied with the amount of weight you've lost

**Phase 1, part 1 (two or more weeks):**

What to eat:

- NO "white," "beige," or "brown" foods
- NO fruits
- YES protein foods (meat, poultry, fish, shellfish, fresh cheeses, seitan, tempeh, soy products)
    - portion: the size of your palm, 3x per day
- YES leafy greens and vegetables (preferably raw)
    - portion: as much as you want
- YES nuts and seeds (Raw, unsalted. Peanuts should be roasted.) — *optional*
    - portion: 1/4 cup, up to 2x per day

**Phase 1, part 2 (four or more weeks):**

- NO "white" or "beige" foods
- NO "killer fruits" (calorie bombs)
- YES protein foods
    - portion: gradually decrease, until it's half the size of your palm
- YES leafy greens and vegetables (preferably raw)
    - portion: increase
- YES "brown" foods (cooked whole grains or legumes) — *optional*
    - portion: up to 1/2 cup per day
- YES black, blue, and red fruits — *optional*

- YES apple and citrus fruits — *optional*
    - ⬚ portion: up to two servings per day
- YES tomatoes and avocados — *optional*


**Phase 2: Restoration**

Purpose: continuing weight loss and setting your body up for longevity

Duration: minimum 6 weeks, then until your weight normalizes

What to eat:

- DECREASE protein foods
    - Portion: try to cut your animal proteins down to one meal per day
- INCREASE vegetables
- YES nuts and seeds (small portions) — *optional*
- YES fruits (in moderation) — *optional*
- YES whole grains and legumes (extremely small portions) — *optional*


**Phase 3: Longevity**

Purpose: lasting health

Duration: this is a lifestyle

What to eat:

- YES vegetables, preferably raw (as much as you want)
- MINIMIZE protein foods
- MINIMIZE fruits
- AVOID whole grains
- AVOID legumes

## Unfriendly Foods (Ch. 4)

Vegetables:

- *Cooked* beets, carrots, and corn
- Peas (shelled)
- Root vegetables (parsnips, turnips, rutabagas, celery root)
- Sweet potatoes
- Vegetable juices

"White" foods:

- Sugar and artificial sweeteners
- Cream, milk, mayonnaise, and creamy dressings
- Rice (including white and brown)
- Rice milk and soy milk
- Potatoes
- Pasta
- Flour
- Bread

"Beige" Foods:

- Bagels, pastries, and other bread products or breaded food
- Blended coffee drinks
- Cereals (hot and cold)
- Chips, crackers, cookies
- Deep-fried foods
- Pizza
- Tortillas (flour and corn)

Killer Fruits (calorie bombs):

- Dates
- Mangoes
- Pineapple
- Plantains
- Raisins
- *Ripe* bananas, papayas, and pears
- *Seedless* grapes
- Dried fruit and fruit strips
- Fruit juices

Other foods:

- Alcohol: mixed drinks, white and rose wine, beer, make liquors
- Honey, molasses, maple syrup, corn syrup, and other sweeteners
- Jan, jellies, preserves, and condiments made with sugar
- Soft drinks (including sugar-free and diet)

**Good Oils (Ch. 7)**

Opt for the following green and brown oils in order to bring your omega-3 to omega-6 ratio back to its proper level (and to satisfy your hunger hormone).

"Green" oils:

- Fish oil
- Extra virgin olive oil
- Avocado oil
- Purslane (a common weed)
- Perilla oil

"Brown" oils (are derived from):

- Walnuts
- Flaxseed
- Rapeseed
- Hemp seed

**Suggested Supplements**

- Selenium, cinnamon, or chromium (refer to Ch. 5)
- Probiotics (with prebiotics) (refer to Ch. 5)
- Vitamin E — *make sure it's "mixed vitamin E" or includes d-alpha tocopherols (not dl)* (refer to Ch. 6)
- Vitamin C (refer to Ch. 6)
- Magnesium (refer to Ch. 6)
- Folic Acid (refer to Ch. 6)
- Other B Vitamins (refer to Ch. 6)
- Fish oil — *make sure it's "molecularly distilled"* (refer to Ch. 7)

- Hawthorne berries, olive leaf extract, magnesium, or manganese (refer to Ch. 7)
- Cranberry extract, grape skin extract, grape seed extract, pycnogenols or mushroom extracts (especially reishi, cordyceps, or maitake) (refer to Ch. 7)
- St. John's Wort, SAM-e, or Citromax (aka garcinia cambozola) (refer to Ch. 8)
- CoQ10 (refer to Ch. 10)
- Acetyl-L-carnitine or L-carnitine (refer to Ch. 10)

More info on supplements can be found at www.drgundry.com.

## Hormetic Agents (Ch. 11-12)

The following list contains suggestions for additional ways you can induce hormetic stress. For each, remember: a little is all you need. If you take any of them too far, then they will turn against you and cause new damage.

- Raw foods, especially dark leafy greens
- Vegetables, especially bitter ones
- Calorie optimization
- Exercise
- Fasting
- Alcohol, especially red wine
- Coffee, Tea, and Chocolate (with no milk)
- Extreme external temperatures
- Vitamins, minerals, and supplements

**Fitness Resources (Ch. 10)**

- The Power of Ten, by Adam Zickerman
- The Slow Burn Fitness Revolution, by Fredrick Hahn

**Helpful Reminders and Rules of Thumb**

Go slow.

1. Lose weight slowly (at an average rate of one pound per week) in order to prevent your body from being overwhelmed by the toxins that are being released from the fat cells that are melting away.
2. Ease yourself into each transition as needed. Gradually decrease sweeteners by "pinching the packet." The transition from mostly protein to more raw greens slowly over time. Start small and work your way up.

When you hit a plateau, settle in. Practice what it takes to maintain a lowered rate. As your body adjusts, the weight loss will pick back up. Weight loss is not like clockwork.

Vary your veggies. This not only delivers a wider array of micronutrients but also keeps your meals more interesting.

The downside to animal protein: Digesting animal protein generates a lot of internal heat, indicating to your genetic autopilot that you're terribly inefficient at burning fuel and working harder than you should be — and therefore aren't of many benefits to the species.

Eat like a gorilla. A 400-pound male silverback gorilla consumes 16 pounds of leaves a day, but only 3% of his body composition is fat. He's pure muscle mass, all generated from leaves.

Our ancestors lifted, pulled, wrestled, and sprinted after things. They also walked long distances. The more you duplicate these actions, the more your genes will identify your behavior as a successful animal.

Aim for at least 60% raw. Embrace your inner Vegephile and build a new happier, healthier you.

Even herbivores need 6% animal protein in their diet. (They usually get this in the form of grubs, worms, and insects found on the leaves they eat.)

Do what you can, where you are, with what you have.

90% of your existing cells are replaced every three months. By giving your genes the right new materials with which to construct your cellular components, you can rapidly build a "new you" — and it's never too late to start.

## More books from Smart Reads

Summary of the Case for Keto by Gary Taubes
Summary of Eat Smarter by Shawn Stevenson
Summary of 4 Hour Body by Tim Ferriss
Summary of Exercised by David E. Lieberman
Summary of End Your Carb Confusion by Eric C. Westman
    with Amy Berger
Summary of Fast This Way by Dave Asprey
Summary of Dr. Kellyann's Bone Broth Diet by Dr. Kellyann
    Petrucci
Summary of Permission to Feel by Dr. Marc Brackett
Summary of Unwinding Anxiety by Judson Brewer
Summary of Set Boundaries, Find Peace by Nedra Glover
    Tawwab
Summary of The Complete Guide to Fasting by Jason Fung
    with Jimmy Moore
Summary of The Diabetes Code by Jason Fung
Summary of The Obesity Code by Jason Fung
Summary of A Radical Awakening by Dr. Shefali Tsabary

## Thank You

Hope you've enjoyed your reading experience.

We here at Smart Reads will always strive to deliver to you the highest quality guides.

So I'd like to thank you for supporting us and reading until the very end.

Before you go, would you mind leaving us a review on Amazon?

It will mean a lot to us and support us creating high quality guides for you in the future.

Thanks once again!

Warmly yours,

The Smart Reads Team

# Download Your Free Gift

As a way to say "Thank You" for being a fan of our series, I've included a free gift for you:

Brain Health: How to Nurture and Nourish Your Brain For Top Performance

Go to www.smart-reads.com to get your FREE book.

The Smart Reads Team